Think!

Retooling Your Mind for Kingdom Success

Written by
Dr. Edward Donalson, III

PublishAmerica
Baltimore

First printing

Hardcover 978-1-4489-3231-3
Softcover 978-1-4489-5446-9
PUBLISHED BY PUBLISHAMERICA, LLLP
www.publishamerica.com
Baltimore

Printed in the United States of America

Nadine C. Keels and Shelia A. O'Connor, Co-Editors

I would like to dedicate this book to my lovely wife, Lady Ujima Donalson. Our quiet-time conversations unlock the genius in me. You know how to push me to purpose I am glad to share this life journey with you. Thanks for being with me in the sunshine and rain.

I would also like to dedicate this book to my parents who taught me the value of the human mind; Overseer Edward Donalson Jr. and Mother Beverly Donalson instilled in me that my mind is a powerful tool and gift given by God to be used to build His Kingdom.

Finally I would like to dedicate this book to my sons and daughters. The reason why I do what I do is to leave a legacy in the earth. I pray that some part of you is blessed by our passage together through this human experience on our way to the eternal presence of the Great King!

Introduction

Recently, my wife went back to graduate school to earn her masters degree in adult education. One night while she and I were lying in bed, discussing the events of that evening's class, she brought up a word that captivated my attention in a way that was more than etymological intrigue. I knew immediately that the Holy Spirit had arrested my mind and there would be much investigation around this concept. The word was "metacognition." The moment the word left her lips, it was as if it bounced off the walls of the room and landed squarely in my spirit. Metacognition refers to a level of thinking that involves active control over the process of thinking, which is used in learning situations. The basic concept of metacognition is thinking about the way you or others think. Planning the way to approach a learning task, monitoring comprehension, and evaluating the progress towards the completion of a task—these are skills that are all metacognitive in their nature.

For days I pondered this function of the mind, realizing that in this hour of time it is not enough for us to just go through our daily routine, thinking the thoughts we have always thought. As God is moving the Church back to its glory and positioning His people to be pivotal in every area of the marketplace, we must begin to scrutinize and know why we think the thoughts we think. What is the driving force behind our behaviors? What are our motivators? What are the thought processes that hinder us from being successful to the fullest extent of our potential? Am I limiting myself by not feeding my mind the diet necessary to be the champion that God made me? These questions began to swim through my mind and connect with what I had discovered in the Bible over my years of study. The simple truth is the path to success starts with a thought process shaped by the Word of God. This book is designed to unlock the potential for greatness that has been hiding inside of you by causing you to purposefully inform the hard drive of your spirit with the spiritual software that is compatible with your destiny. No more can negativity rule in the lives of Kingdom citizens. It is time for us to put on the mind of Christ! Our thoughts have caused us to be stuck in cycles of frustration because we have refused to break out of old paradigms and comfort zones.

We are living in an hour in the history of the world where secular thought has no answer to the questions that are relevant to the daily lives of the world's citizens. The problems of the world have reached critical mass; from the streets of the United States to Sierra Leone, the crisis cannot be handled by conventional western thought. It is prime time for the Church to rise up with Kingdom answers and yet we are, for the most part, an impotent sleeping giant. Completely unaware that the window of opportunity to have a seat at the table of the marketplace and to bring the thoughts of the Heavens into manifestation in the earth realm is already closing, we are immobilized because we have not taken the time to think! Like Daniel and his con padres in his time, there is an anointing in the earth realm now to bring Zion to Babylon and to show them that God reigns in the Kingdom of men and He "giveth" it to whomsoever He will. I challenge you to take the journey of reformation of the mind and release your inner world changer.

Proverbs 23:7a gives us important insight on the power of thought. It says, "*For as he thinketh in his heart, so is he.*"[1] In this text, we discover that the Jewish concept of thought is *sha'ar,* which means: to split open, reason out, calculate, reckon, or estimate.[2] This very definition reveals that our responsibility as believers is to split open our own thought process and reason out the driving force behind what makes us who we are. Our thoughts originate on the core of our being; they are from our heart. The author of this text uses the word *nephesh,* which connotes "soul, self, life, creature, person, appetite, mind, living being, desire, emotion, or passion." It also connotes "that which breathes the breathing substance or being, soul, the inner being of man."[3] Your thoughts literally reveal who you are! Just think for a moment what your day would be like if everyone that passed by knew the content of your thoughts on any particular subject. What would be different about your relationships if people could see even a portion of what really makes you an individual?

You are what you think you are, so you must ask yourself, "What can I become if I change my thought? The reason I am a new creature in Christ is because my thought process and worldview changes, hence my behavior and the consequences of said behaviors also change. Changing one's mind not only changes the effects of the world around you, but it equally changes your effect on it. I have become increasingly convinced that if the Church will pour the right thoughts into its constituents, they will rise up and see a manifestation of the Kingdom on earth like at no other point in history. The following pages are what I see as seeds of reformation of the mind and the genesis of genius. You and I determine the quality of soil and what the seed will produce. Let us journey together to the place of greatness.

This book is meant to be read as a daily devotional: one chapter per day, or one in the morning and one in the evening, to stimulate thought and activate metacognition. At the end of each section, there is a small subdivision entitled "Moment of Clarity" designed to help focus your prayer around the concept found in that section. I pray that you will leave this book completely refueled with passion and renewed in the mind. My writing this book comes not out of a need to fill the marketplace with yet another volume of dribble, but rather out of a deep love for the people of God. I pray that your destiny and calling can be activated, and that your thoughts of success will be stirred to overflowing as you navigate my heart with regards to the Biblical mandate of thought.

I would like to take a moment to introduce you to one of the greatest minds in the world of Christendom. Elder Elect Darrick Keels. He is my son in the Gospel and one of the greatest thinkers of this generation. I asked Him to share with you his thoughts on this book in hopes that his testimonial would incite you to do the work of retooling what is needed in your life. Each of us needs role models and paradigms to push us to purpose and it is my prayer that these words can begin empowering you in that way. Look for more to come from Elder Elect Keels and know that as you are reading his words, you are getting a glimpse into the mind of the leaders on the edge of the court calling out "We got next!"

The Testimony:

This book is phenomenal. The process of retooling my mind was definitely initiated after reading through Apostle Donalson's writing. Becoming aware of my own thought process as it relates to ministry, family, work, and even myself has changed my life dramatically. I was not aware that there were so many strongholds that I was operating under, many of which were holding me back from reaching my potential in various areas of my life. For example, now when I look at my goals for my business, I have to ask myself if every area of my business is operating in accordance to the laws of the Kingdom. I have to ask myself before implementing a new system in my ministry if it is a system that reflects the systems of God.

I have believed for some time now that I have the ability to be ten times better than the world in every aspect of my life because I understand how the Bible says in Daniel, that Daniel and his friends were ten times better than those who were operating under the system of Babylon. However, after reading through *Think*, I realized that much of being ten times better in the marketplace has much to do with the way I think. Daniel truly believed that the diet of God, although not popular, would lead to better results than consuming the king's meat and wine. Daniel actually told his boss to test him and see if his system would be better than the traditional Babylonian system. He had confidence because he understood the systems of God. I have begun retooling my mind and changing various mental audio tapes that have been playing in my head for so many years. I feel empowered to infiltrate the marketplace with the counter culture of the Kingdom and be successful at it. I will no longer make decisions based on false evidence, but have full confidence in the evidence God gives in His Word.

Think has even caused me to read the Bible from a different vista. I look for the Word of God to activate my thought life. I know that there are things the Lord has already put inside of me but it takes the water of the Word and the breath of God to bring life to the passions, desires, and gifts that have been lying dormant in me. I see the Word of God as more than a guide for life that teaches you the do's and don'ts of a system. I see the Word of God as God's tool to change the way I think. I realize now more than ever that life is often what I think it is. If I change my thoughts, I literally change my life. Situations do not suddenly change, but I do change in the situation. I no longer try to change situations. Many situations cannot be changed by me but I can control the way I view a situation. I see struggles as areas of opportunity. Anywhere there is a struggle in my life I see it as an opportunity for victory. After changing my thought process I can see opportunity in the gravest of situations. I look at circumstance as a way for God to flex and show off His power through me right in the middle of a rough spot.

The visual vista in which I see the world has changed because my thoughts have changed. Sight is based on the mind. And now that my mind has new tools in the tool box, my sight is new. The vision for my life is now 20/20. The vision for my business is 20/20. It does not matter what the weather forecast is because I have the tools in my life to navigate the various weather conditions that come with different seasons. I challenge every reader of this book to use this book to put fuel in your think tank. It is time for the people of God to change the way they *THINK!*

Chapter 1
Higher Thoughts

From that time Jesus began to preach, and to say, Repent: for the kingdom of heaven is at hand.[4]

Matthew 4:17

Jesus comes on the scene and begins His earthly message by echoing the sentiments of His forerunner, preaching the gospel of the Kingdom, but He frames it in a particular context: it is the framework of repentance. For years in the Church, I had a limited understanding of this concept because I thought it was synonymous with confession. I was under the impression that whenever I had committed a sin or done something less than the standard of God, as I would apologize to whomever I had wronged and then to Him, I was repenting. The truth is that Christ had a very different idea of what repentance is. The word used in this text is *metanoeo,* which means "to change one's mind for better." The truth of repentance is that it has nothing to do with confession and everything to do with a change in one's mentality. If we understand that when the Scriptures speak of strongholds, they are really referring to a system of thought, then we can embrace repentance as the process of divorcing oneself from a system of thought.

Christ communicates to us in this text that in order to embrace the Kingdom of God you must first have an upgrade in your thinking. Before we can go any further in our process of metacognition and engage in a discussion about our thoughts, we must meet at the foot of the cross in a place of earnest repentance asking God to help us upgrade our thought process. We must divorce ourselves from our previous morés and new mandates must become the infrastructure of our decision making process. Kingdom living is a life of abundance and wealth (financial wealth is only a minuscule portion of the overall picture of true Kingdom wealth), but it cannot be pursued through the vehicle of mediocrity. It must come from the vast expanse of a regenerated mind.

As I pondered this truth in my pursuit of thought, I had to wrestle with the fact that I had not truly repented in many areas of my life because I had not upgraded my thoughts in specific areas of concern.

The next portion of the definition of *metaneono* is: "to heartily amend with abhorrence of one's past sins."[5] Now I am looking at my thoughts in action. As I change my mind about a given topic, there is an expectation of corresponding behavior, which is the fruit of my thoughts. Just as my counter Kingdom thoughts had previously produced behavior that was destructive or kept me from the fullness of my privilege in Christ, so the new thought processes produce in me an elevation in Kingdom productivity. Change is impossible until I reject the old system of thought to embrace the new infrastructure.

Moment of Clarity: Today, take a moment and ask the Spirit of the Lord to reveal to you areas of repentance in your life. Ask yourself, "Where do I need an upgrade in my system of thought?" As the Lord begins to reveal to your heart areas in which you need His spirit to bring your thoughts into alignment with the message of the Kingdom, make a commitment to finding empowerment resources to help you reinforce or give shape to that Kingdom thought process. If your struggle is to see your finances from a Kingdom perspective, make a commitment to purchase a book on finance, or attend a seminar/workshop around stewardship principles. The only way to see the Kingdom manifest in your area of opportunity is to make a commitment to change your mind and plan to produce corresponding actions.

Chapter 2
The Power of the Seed

Now the parable is this: The seed is the word of God.[6]
Luke 8:11

The parable of the sower is one of the more well known parables in Christian circles. Preachers of every theological stream and ecumenical source love to pontificate about how people receive the Word of God, and even more, they joy in preaching about the types of people who do not. I am afraid however that the truth, simplicity, and brilliance of the text is lost through the venting of frustrated prognosticators of the Gospel. This text connotes such a pure strain of truth that begs to be explored when, in an almost oversimplification of eternity, Christ declares that the seed is the Word of God.

The Kingdom and all of the genius attached to us comes to us not as steak and potatoes, but rather it comes in capsule size servings that empower us to achieve greatness; it comes in seed form. God puts the word in concept, waiting for it to hit the human spirit where it germinates. This is known as conception, and then once concept meets soul, it produces fruit known as manifestation. Your concepts (thoughts) determine the manifestation. By now you should be actively engaged in the conversation with the lines written in the pages of this book to maximize your growth.

If a seed is not allowed to germinate within a certain period of time, that seed will die. Some seeds have incredibly long life expectancy. However, others have a relatively short season of viability. While the maple species need to sprout within two weeks, there are some lotus plants that have seed viability for up to two thousand years. This can be said of so many concepts and thoughts you have had in your life. Some concepts have to be activated right away or your passion and drive to bring that particular thought to manifestation dissipates, and what once seemed like a stroke of genius now fades into the file known as daydream or fantasy. By the same token, some concepts are so powerful and precious to you that even though the opportunity to act on them takes years to come, as soon as the opportunity presents itself, you spring into action with passion as if the concept came to you for the first time that very morning. As believers, we renew our minds with the concepts of the Kingdom. These become our thoughts, and it is important to know that there is a life expectancy on the thoughts that are released to us and a season for improvement and empowerment.

Just as seed germination originates in the darkness of the earth's soil, life manifestation begins with the darkness of meditation. The concepts or thoughts you meditate on become the substance of your manifestation. I repeat, only because it is worth repeating, that you are what you think. As you meditate on Kingdom concepts and Biblically based wisdom, you will begin to produce the Kingdom and wisdom, because your thoughts, like seeds, were the cause of your greatness. The process of accelerated growth begins in the secret place of your thought life. You must be aware of the truth that everything is created twice, first in the mind and then in the tangible world. What you are able to construct is determined by the kind of thoughts that are supplied in the process of formation.

It is most important to note that Jesus, as He teaches on the power of concept in Luke: 8, is specific about what thoughts are necessary for Kingdom success. The source of these life-giving thoughts is the Word of God. I feel that I must be clear at this juncture and say that this is not another stab at the power of positive thinking. This is a look at the power of the Word of God to transform the thought process of any individual by unlocking the treasure that has been placed inside of each one by the Sovereign Creator of the universe. Indeed we think ourselves to new dimensions and new peaks of performance, but the thoughts must be generated not by our own internal compass, but rather our thoughts must become saturated in the mind of God.

Moment of Clarity: What is informing your thoughts? What do your seeds look like? The higher the quality of seed, the greater the potential for outstanding fruit. So, ask yourself if you are satisfied with the fruit that your life bears, and whether or not there is an issue with the seed. Ask the Lord to prepare your heart to be soil that is rich and ready to receive the higher quality of seed He wants to be sown into your life. In the past five years of my life, I have undergone a major spiritual renovation so that my soil can handle higher quality seed. As I dealt with myself and positioned myself to receive, God began to drop concepts into my spirit that have revolutionized my world. My prayer for you is that you will learn to be blessed with God's choicest seed!

Chapter 3
Thought Exchange

And be renewed in the spirit of your mind…
Ephesians 4:23

The interesting thing to me about metacognition is that it is something most people, and notably most Christians, no longer give any time to. As I read writings from older civilizations and schools of thought other than Western protestant authors, I notice a continuous wrestling, not only with current thought, but with the root or cause of that thought. This type of mental dialog has been done away with in much of today's modernity, and yet it has always held a fascination for me. It has forever seemed to me that great people think a lot and come to at least a mild understanding of why they think the way they do, and yet so few of us even attempt to analyze the basis for our thoughts. Built on the slippery foundation of presuppositions, we think our thoughts without ever considering the state of our own mental affairs.

As I have searched the Scriptures, I have come to see that for the believer metacognition is a direct command. Earlier in this passage of Scripture, Paul admonishes the church at Ephesus to not walk as other Gentiles in mental vanity. The word in the text is *mataiotes,* which means "what is devoid of truth and appropriateness or frailty, want of vigour."[7] In other words, we are admonished against being believing airheads! The command of God is to be mentally astute and the text indicates that those who do not employ themselves with the business of thought clearly displease our God.

Not only are we challenged to new heights of mental ascent, it is clear from the text that whatever system of thought we are on prior to embracing the truth and power of God is inferior and in need of drastic overhaul. Have you ever stopped to sort through which of your thoughts or thought process were in need of a drastic overhaul and should be submitted to the Holy Spirit for renewal in order to change the scope and direction of your life? Consider for a moment the genius of the Sony Corporation. The founder of Sony started out to accomplish one thing, and that was to change the mind of the world about Japanese products. His success is not measured by the revenue of the company although it is very impressive! His success is measured by the fact that the world buys Sony because we think that Sony makes superior goods, even when the particular product is below industry standards. This is what it means to renew a mind to totally eradicate an old thought and replace it with a new one.

Ephesians 4:23 goes on to make the connection for us that transformation begins with the mind. The question we must ask ourselves if we are to really engage in true metacognition is what is "the mind"? (At least in the writer's thoughts). Paul uses the Greek word *nous,* which means "a particular mode of thinking and judging, i.e. thoughts, feelings, purposes, desires."[8] While there are other connotations to the definition of this word, this is what stood out to me as it relates to the topic at hand. We are not called to continue in blindness or to allow thoughts to drive and motivate us without careful examination of those thoughts. It is not a light thing that our God commands that we adopt a new mode of thinking.

Moment of Clarity: My concern for the Body of Christ today is that we are governed by a set of assumptions and presuppositions that are not always in line with a Biblical worldview. Rather than thinking the thoughts of the Kingdom, many times we succumb to the tenor of our cultural environment, and our thoughts are directed by the norm in the system of Babylon rather than by the Kingdom of Light. Challenge yourself to hold your thoughts on politics, marriage, gay rights, or even immigration, up to the spotlight of the Word, and then ask God to renew your mind in every area that does not line up directly with His Word. This is the foundation of unlocking your brilliance.

Chapter 4
Thinking Out of This Word!

But we have the mind of Christ.
I Corinthians 2:16b

The whole concept of new thought is outlined for us in the second chapter of First Corinthians. Paul speaks of a wisdom that is only available to those who are initiated into the Christian faith. This initiation into faith comes through the process of learning the doctrine of Christ. It is interesting to me that this brilliant scholar and Politian come to the Christian faith only to discover that his thought process until this point was inadequate and immature. Early in the chapter, there is talk about the virtue of a mature mind in concert with the mysteries of God. It is this new thought process that makes one able to see, hear, and know the limitless potential that others whose thoughts have not been elevated by the Word of God, will never be able to ascertain. This is because as believers, we have the capacity for spiritual truth, the higher powers of the soul, and the faculty of perceiving divine things,[9] which comes from the mental integration of the thoughts of Christ.

As you live out the mind of Christ, He makes you like Daniel and his friends. They were ten times better than any of the best in Babylon because their thought processes caused their approach to matters to induce a better outcome. It is important that we understand as believers in Christ that our thoughts are designed by God to produce excellence in our lives.

As citizens of the Kingdom of Heaven living in the system of Babylon, we have a mandate to bring higher thought to our daily surroundings. The captivity of Babylon was especially dangerous for the Jewish people because they were allowed to function culturally, but their spiritual relevance was taken from them. We live in the postmodern age where, for the most part, society global does not care if we maintain a Church culture as long as our spirituality does not become relevant to anything in the mainstream marketplace. The purpose of the mind of Christ is not to sit idly by and watch the world happen around us. Christ's mind is to empower us to excellence, to push us to purpose, and to create the environment of creativity that will position us to dominate, subjugate, and rule the world around us.

It is not just any thought process we are gaining; it is the mind of Christ the Messiah, the Son of God, the Sovereign Creator of all that is, depositing the thought process in us that made the universe. Out of absolutely nothing comes all things that are, and then, through Christ, He transmits this creative power to us through the acknowledgement of the principles of truth that are found, not only in the sacred text, but also in moments of quiet meditation. These are the moments when He reveals the depths of His love for you, and your own character is stripped away to reveal that, at your core, the love of God is shed abroad.

Moment of Clarity: For a moment, imagine yourself with limitless power and infinite potential. What would you do? What would you build? What system would you introduce into the earth realm? These are the thoughts of greatness, the sparks of revolution, and the fuel that can change the world. Why continue in the bondage of mediocrity when the dimension of greatness is waiting for you? Ask yourself if the fuel of your thought process is meting out the unlimited wealth of potential in your life, or if your thoughts are keeping you in a box that prevents you from breaking into new spheres of influence that are awaiting your arrival. Ask the Lord to enlarge the territory of your mind and to saturate your thinking with His Glory.

Chapter 5
Your Crop Is In

Be not deceived; God is not mocked: for whatsoever a man soweth, that shall he also reap.[10]
Galatians 6:7

I believe that thoughts govern all behavior. What we believe we will ultimately produce, and this concept has come to pass in my personal life many times. All through my educational experience, my parents instilled in me a philosophy that I could do anything I set my mind to. This "you can do it" mentality was backed up by the best education money could buy in a private school, but the school did not share the same philosophy of empowerment, and the social climate of the institution did not agree with me. This school had no faculty or staff that looked like me, and for the better part of my education, it had no students from my same ethnic background either. There I was introduced to the thought that my options for life were possibly limited. In fact, I was told that perhaps I should attend a vocational school because I would never be successful in a four year college. Battered and broken from the structure of what was designed to help, I bought into the thought process that I did not have the goods to make it at a four year college, and my freshman year, I received horrible grades.

That year I moved back to Seattle and began working on a two year degree at an institute, which I completed. After working in the marketplace for several years, I decided to go back and pursue further education. I earned both a Bachelor and a Masters degree with the greatest of ease, and the only things that ever changed were the tapes that played in my mind. During my first year of college, the only tape I heard playing was the prophet of gloom and doom telling me that success would be forever a stranger to me in that educational context. My second attempt at furthering my education was fueled by my original tapes, which declared with wild abandon that I could do anything.

The moment I switched the seed, I began to see signs of harvest. I started doing very well, and in fact I earned all A's in my first classes in seminary. Nothing about me had changed except the posture of my mindset. Finally, the message of my earliest days of life had hit the soil of my soul. I could do it! There wasn't anyone or anything that could hold me back because my mind was towards pleasing God and producing something in my life that would glorify Him and advance the Kingdom.

I learned through this process a very practical power of the seed of your thoughts: whatever thoughts are driving you, you will reap the harvest of that seed. The Scripture is clear: whatever you sow, you will reap. Our thoughts and the thoughts sown into the mind of others are the embryos of either success or failure. It took the seed a while to manifest, but the thought process placed in my spirit by my parents brought a great harvest. The night of my graduation, my parents sat proudly watching their seeds come to full maturity; after struggling through my high school years and watching me doubt my own abilities, finally, I had come full circle to a graduate degree. What a joy it was to see their faces light up with excitement as what they knew was true all along manifested in their very presence.

Moment of Clarity: What negative thought process in you is an ideological seed planted by someone else that has cropped up in your garden? Why have you adopted a view about yourself contrary to the truth of your genius? What situations and circumstances in your life have formed negative opinions about what you can and cannot do? Ask the Lord to change your vista about your future. There is inside of you a great abundance of potential and promise. My prayer for you is that the tapes of your subconscious mind will match the prescription of the Heavens for love and good works in your life.

Chapter 6
No Fear Here

For the thing which I greatly feared is come upon me, and that which I was afraid of is come unto me.[11]
Job 3:25

Recently I preached a message called "The Fruit of Fear". It came from a study of Job, who lost everything he had, including his children who died all in one place in one day. A further study of Job indicates that prior to the death of his children, he would often make sacrifices on their behalf in case they happened to offend God. I see in Job's actions a fault line and an open door for the enemy's attack. The place of his fear was the source of his pain. This is so simple and yet so overlooked.

When Satan went up before God, he received permission from God to attack Job, and yet Job was said to be perfect (mature) and upright. Since God is a God of order and law, I had to find a legal entry point for Satan to invade the covering of God. I had to discover what activated God to give permission for the covering to be removed. Then I stumbled, almost by accident, onto this verse in Job 3:25; Job had the answer to his own dilemma. He was operating in fear, and that was the entry point for the attack of the enemy.

It is as plain as the nose on your face: *But without faith it is impossible to please him: for he that cometh to God must believe that he is, and that he is a rewarder of them that diligently seek him* (Hebrews 11:6). Fear and faith cannot occupy the same space, and the reward of fear is the manifestation of what is feared. Hope is the seed of faith, according to Hebrews 11:1 "Now faith is the substance of things hoped for, the evidence of things not seen," and hope becomes the springboard to manifestation. Fear is a form of hope; it is the negative side of what could be, and just like its positive counterpart, it brings to us a manifestation of itself. Like faith, fear too bears its own rewards.

Most people, whether cognitively or not, bring a certain set of assumptions to any given situation in life, and without any thought, those assumptions are either fear based or faith based. These core assumptions bring to bear a manifestation of their seed. How many times have you approached something with fear, only to have the experience confirm you were right in doubting? Conversely, how many times have you approached, with great faith, what seemed to others to be an impossible situation, and to the amazement of yourself and others, met great success? There is a Kingdom concept: your thoughts must be full of faith.

Moment of Clarity: Activate metacognition about the root source of your thoughts. Ask yourself if you are living in faith or fear. Are you producing in your life continual bench marks on your path to destiny, or are you sitting on the bench watching destiny pass you by? Take some time to pray, then analyze where your faith is strong and where you are operating in fear. Make a commitment to right thinking and focus in on what God has already said about you. My prayer for you is that your faith will increase and that your fears will dissipate into the eternal abyss; that your soul and thoughts would be filled with the mind of God toward you and all that pertains to you.

Chapter 7
Visionary Thinking

Without a Vision is a people made naked, and whoso is keeping the law, O his happiness![12]

Proverbs 29:18

Many messages have been preached from this text, yet there are still visionless citizens in the Kingdom, some of which even have the audacity to hold leadership positions in the house of God. So I pause to share about the faculties of vision with you. Visual perception is the ability to interpret visible light information reaching the eyes, which is then made available for planning and action. The spiritual counterpart to this is that vision is the act of interpreting information that is held up to the Light, which is Christ Jesus!

As I began to comprehend what Solomon spoke about as he wrote on the topic of vision, I started to realize that vision is produced by an understanding of God. You cannot separate God from His Word ("In the beginning was the Word, and the Word was with God, and the Word was God")[13], which in Old Testament times was known as the Law. Vision is then produced by an understanding of the Law of God and its function in your life. When the Word is investigated properly and applied to the life of the believer, vision is then engendered.

The thought process of a person with vision begins and ends with the Word of God. The more you fill your mind with His Word, the clearer His vision comes forth in your life. In the pursuit of reaching happiness, thinking about the concepts of the Kingdom is the foundation of the process. The Kingdom of God is a counterculture to the kingdom of this world, and the focus of God's Kingdom is the glory of the King. The King has set laws in the Kingdom for the benefit of His royal subjects whom

He has seen fit to adopt as sons. Each citizen of the Kingdom is then an heir of the King and all of His domain, and is officially a Prince. As long as the King's laws are honored, Kingdom success comes as a right of position.

Moment of Clarity: Will you govern your thought process according to the laws of the Kingdom? How many of us have given ourselves wholly to investigating and understanding the laws of the Kingdom of God? When is the last time you washed your thoughts with the power of the Word? Is your thought life dedicated to furthering your understanding of the laws of God? Seek the Lord in prayer today and purposefully submit your thoughts to the laws of God. Spend ten minutes in the Word of God and look for Scriptures related to your greatest area of struggle. Then commit yourself to memorizing those Scriptures and making the changes communicated through them. My prayer for you is that God will grant you all wisdom as you search His Word to find His Law and apply it to your thoughts.

Chapter 8
The Right Esteem

For I say, through the grace given to me, to everyone who is among you, not to think of himself more highly than he ought to think, but to think soberly, as God has dealt to each one a measure of faith.

Romans 12:3

It is interesting in this generation of self-esteem workshops and self-help gurus that when the Sacred Text mentions self-esteem, it comes in the form of an admonition rather than an approval. In Western thought, feeling and thinking "only what is wonderful" has become the hallmark of emotional health. People are wandering through life and taught only to see and think the best of themselves at the cost of looking realistically and introspectively with an eye to becoming better. It amazes me that all the emotional health that this is supposed to promote only serves to engender more greed, lust, and corruption. We have lied to our children, telling them they can do or be anything, while ignoring obvious challenges and real circumstances that prevent them from achieving certain goals, that would never ultimately bring them fulfillment.

While I do believe that we are challenged to value ourselves as Kingdom citizens, I am not sure that we have rightly discerned what that really looks like in the eyes of God. The thought process of self-esteem in the Kingdom is that we must come to our self-image with an accurate assessment of who and what we are. The way to a better you starts not with visioning the "you" that you want to be; it begins with discovering who you are.

I am convinced that the next generation of world-changing geniuses is made up of people who understand their personal strengths and weaknesses. This emerging generation of leaders is a group of people who have given themselves to times of pensive reflection that goes past the obvious gifts and talents to an investigation of the depths of their souls. There must be a daring group of people who will burst on the scene that have given themselves to perfecting their areas of potential, rather than spending years trying to prove that they can master the area that is furthest from greatness.

As we think about self-esteem or self-evaluation, we must understand that proper self-esteem is not seeing ourselves as wonderful, but rather it is seeing ourselves as we are in truth and allowing the Light of Christ to make us better. We must begin putting our energy behind a realistic vista of the potential of the best we can be. By avoiding the comparison trap and using our brain power to concentrate on cultivating the greatness of God within us.

Moment of Clarity: What do I have to offer that the world is waiting for? What area is the path I should take to express the greatness of God? In what areas am I least likely to produce quality fruit, and why am I giving my time and attention to them? The Lord wants you to have a realistic view of who you are so that you can express His image to all of creation. Are you focused, and how are your thoughts playing into a misperception of yourself? My prayer for you is that God will grant you clarity as it pertains to your strengths and weaknesses, and to what will bring you the greatest harvest in the Kingdom.

Chapter 9
We Are at WAR!

And I behold another law in my members, warring against the law of my mind, and bringing me into captivity to the law of the sin that is in my members.[14]
Romans 7:23

Paul speaks in this text from Romans about the struggle that we have, as followers of Christ, between our sinful nature and our regenerated mind. In the same passage he speaks about the good that he wants to do being the opposite of what he ends up doing, and the evil that he does not wish to commit being easily manifested. Herein lies the struggle we all face: our Kingdom thoughts at war with our sinful nature. The book of 1 John says "If we say that we have no sin, we deceive ourselves, and the truth is not in us." (1:8)[15] Now this word "sin" literally means "that which is done wrong; sin; an offence; a violation of the divine law in thought or in act."[16] In other words, it is the inward element (thought) that produces acts of offence to God. When the author Paul speaks of this great internal struggle, he is really talking about the battle of the mind, the struggle for what his thoughts are and what they will ultimately produce.

Most of us think that where we are in life is the result of a random set of situations and circumstances rather than the results of the thoughts we have allowed to dominate the landscape of our minds. Whatever place you are in at his exact moment in your life, you thought yourself here! Whether you have had thoughts of righteousness or unrighteousness, your life has manifested the seeds your mind has sown. How many of us are willing to come to grips with this reality: "I am culpable for my life status because my thought process has brought me here. Whether it is wrong thinking about finance and accountability that has brought me to a place of poverty, or not placing importance on education being the reason I have no degree, it has all been a matter of my thoughts. There is no external conspiracy holding me in this socioeconomic stratum, only a lack of information that will change my thoughts and elevate my situation?"

Paul's struggle in the text, Romans 7:23, is that he clearly understands that he has two distinct and opposing systems of thought working simultaneously in his mind, and the responsibility for these thoughts rests squarely on his shoulders. So, if thoughts got us into negative places, then conversely, thoughts can get us out and on top! What a wonderful redemptive moment to know that turning things around is possible if only we inform ourselves of the thoughts of God concerning every area of our lives. The struggle is to surrender my mind to a pattern of thoughts that will ultimately lead me to success. There is no secret formula that only a hand-selected group of people have access to that will make ready a happy life, but there are some distinct thought processes that make a manifestation of success more than probable for those who will dare to do the work of retooling the mind.

Moment of Clarity: Reseed the garden of your life with thoughts of success. Stop living in fear and doubt about what you can or cannot accomplish. Stand on the foundational Biblical principles that you know are accurate and right. What has been a conflict for you in your old paradigm of thought? Begin today to investigate what the fruit your thoughts bring to bear in your life, and make a firm commitment to planting new seed. My prayer for you is that as you begin to check the fruit of your life, God will reveal to you the seed of thought that is producing what is good, as well as what is rotten, fruit. I pray that as you discover the source of the bad seed, you will quickly sift it out and begin to sow good seed in the fertile soil of your life.

Chapter 10
Focus

A double minded man is unstable in all his ways.
James 1:8

The Greek word for double minded is *dipsuchos* which means "wavering, uncertain, doubting or divided in interest."[17] A common understanding of the term double minded is the ability of a man to affix his heart on two opposing goals simultaneously. In other words, we want to have our cake and eat it too, to employ an overused American folk saying. James has hit on a major dilemma for most of us when we begin to actively engage in metacognition. If we are honest with ourselves, many of the thoughts we think are fundamentally opposed to other thoughts we hold to be equal in validity.

The raw truth is that many of our thoughts do not fit within our own circle of reason. This becomes painfully apparent when we are forced to share our thoughts with others, and it becomes clear that no justifiable connection can resolve the contradiction in the path of our thoughts. Ready to go to war with those who do not see our version of "common sense," we shrink pathetically into isolation, feeling justified in saying that our thoughts are obvious but no one is listening to us or no one understands us. We stay in this pity party of isolation until someone with an equally distorted view comes along and justifies our mental dysfunction, but all the while in the back of our minds and hearts, there is a knowing feeling of what the truth is: we simply do not make logical sense. The hardest part about coming to the realization that my own thoughts conflict is deciding what level of dysfunction I am willing to tolerate out of me. For many of us, the choice is never one thought or the other, but rather it is, "How do I reconcile these two opposing views and maintain both?"

For those of us who really wish to be Christ-like and whole in our lives and productivity, this division within ourselves must be resolved. If double mindedness leads to instability, it cannot be tolerated on any level. At some point, the integration of thoughts is necessary for us to be whole. Could it be the hindrance to progress in some areas of your life has to do with some place of double mindedness? For example, there could be a groom who loves his fiancé and longs for wedded bliss while secretly yearning for the carefree days of single life. This seriously impedes the progress of the relationship because the measure of double mindedness prevents clarity of focus and vision.

In many of our lives, the greatness of the next season, or even the next step, is being held up only by the fact that our thoughts are not single in their focus and vision, causing major instability to affect the way we see others and the way we are seen by others. If we could ever bring our thoughts into alignment, our destination would be assured and the path to arrive at it would be made straight. In reviewing the whole of the passage in James, I have come to the conclusion that the only way to receive anything from God is to integrate your thoughts by allowing your thoughts to be His.

Moment of Clarity: In how many areas of your life do you have double minded tendencies? What are the things that cause you the most grief when it comes to reconciling your thoughts? Are there any areas of your life where progress is being held up because you simply cannot bring yourself to focus on what God says about a given thought process? I am sure that if we put our minds to it, we can track down areas in our lives where we exhibit some form of double mindedness, and we must repent for those areas. My prayer for you is that God will grant you the courage to reconcile your thoughts and to embrace His thoughts concerning you!

Chapter 11
The Power of Relationship

Can two walk together, except they be agreed?
Amos 3:3

The process of changing one's mindset is not done in isolation, just as life does not happen on an island. Everything happens in the context of relationship. When thinking about one's thoughts and thought processes, one has to also take into consideration what has influence over the way one thinks. There should be clarity about who has permission to address and influence your thought process. When the people you associate with validate your wrong thinking, it makes it virtually impossible to pull yourself out of the cycle of continuing that thought pattern. After identifying wrong thinking, the next step is imperative. You must identify who you are connected to who thinks the same way you do about the situation at hand. The people who have voice in your life feed the seed of your thoughts, and whatever pattern of thoughts you are currently in, the people closest to you have a similar pattern going on in their lives.

The road to producing great, new results starts with great, new thoughts. There are many new thoughts that old connections simply cannot embrace. It is difficult to begin the process of letting people go, but in order to protect the seed of the Word, it is crucial for you to surround yourself with people who are thinking correctly. A moment of truth is this: after you have identified wrong thinking and those who contribute to it, the next step is to identify right thinking and those who contribute to it.

Connect yourself to people who have the fruit of right thinking showing in their lives in the same area you are trying to correct. Do not be afraid to admit you need help thinking clearly or like Christ on a particular matter, and be ready to receive the deposit of wisdom they may impart to you. Right thinking is a result of being positioned in the place to receive the mind of Christ with regards to a subject. You must surround yourself with people who are surrendered to God as the source of the seed of thought.

I am aware that old habits die hard and people many times will not allow you to move on without judgments about why you are moving or who you are. Sometimes these hasty conclusions hurt, especially when the people making them have once walked in close relationship with us. However, it is too expensive to hold on to seeds that no longer produce the fruit that is the desired goal.

Moment of Clarity: Who is attached to me that keeps me hanging on to my old system of unproductive thought? Who do I know that exhibits the fruit I wish to show in my life? Am I attached to the right people to advance in the Kingdom? Take a few moments and reflect on your dominant relationships, to evaluate the type of seed that is exchanged in your relationships. My prayer for you is that God will grant you Kingdom connections that will deposit the right seed in your life.

Chapter 12
Dealing with the Heart of Me!

Lo, truth Thou hast desired in the inward parts, And in the hidden part Wisdom Thou causest me to know.[18]

Psalms 51:6

The idea of thinking about our own thought process is new to most of us. This new idea is met with both joy and some amount of trepidation, because as wonderful as it may seem to embrace one's thoughts, it is equally scary considering most of us do not have a clue as to why we do what we do. In order to change our thought process or even to evaluate the ones we currently have, it will require brutal honesty with ourselves.

Honesty with oneself can at times be the most difficult of all honest, because it requires us to be objective about things we are emotionally attached to. The questions it raises challenge us to become better people and to deal with the fact that we are not the person we thought we were, nor are we in most cases the person we hoped we would be. The challenge of metacognition is deciding what to do when I come to grips with who I am. Once I discover who I am, am I willing to do the work to become what I have identified as right?

This call to radical honesty is different for each individual because we live in varying degrees of denial, and coming to grips with the raw truth about us may take longer for some than for others. The real challenge is not identifying the thought patterns and processes that govern our day to day lives or business affairs; it is identifying the overarching motivator of the thought process. Coming to the realization that you discriminate against a particular people group is not the challenge, but rather it is coming to grips with why you tolerate that discrimination in your life.

There was a young man that I once had an amicable relationship with, and most people would have referred to us as friends. The relationship deteriorated over time, and being in his presence began to gnaw at my insides. Someone who had once been a friend turned into a bitter enemy. There was so much anger and distain inside of me that I could not stand to be in the same room as him for extended periods of time. I thought of all the reasons to justify my passionate dislike of him and even had a list that gave me Godly reasons why it was righteous indignation. Then, one day the Spirit of the Lord spoke gently to me that the reason I hated this man was that I had the potential to become like him. Now that is honest.

This is the type of raw honesty necessary for Kingdom citizens to make honest assessments of their own hearts. Nothing changes for the better when we are afraid to honestly analyze what is in our hearts. When is the last time you asked yourself the "why" behind how you thought or felt about a person or situation? When was the last conversation among you and your friends not about the consensus, but rather about the motive behind the common thought?

Moment of Clarity: Ask yourself about the motive attached to your thought process and about how honest you are concerning your thoughts. Are there areas of self-deception that must come to the surface to bring our cognition into the right posture in the Kingdom? My prayer for you is that the Word of God will separate the thought from the intent of your heart, and that God will purify your motives in every area of your life so that there is no hindrance in embracing the thought pattern of the Heavens.

Chapter 13
Ready for Battle

For the weapons of our warfare are not fleshly, but powerful to God for bringing down of strongholds,[19]

2 Corinthians 10:4

This is indeed a powerful text, in light of the past decade of teaching on spiritual warfare that has swept the global Church. Every ministry office in the Body of Christ has had within its ranks those who have made equipping us to do battle with the kingdom of darkness their personal mission. Satan and all of his minions have become characters of epic proportions responsible for everything negative and anything that does not jive with our comfortableness. It is not that I am in any way a fan or supporter of Satan. However I do believe he may be blamed in the modern Church for more than his fair share of things he has no involvement in.

Ochuroma is the Greek word used in 2 Corinthians 10:4 for "stronghold". It means "anything on which one relies or the arguments and reasoning by which a disputant endeavors to fortify his opinion and defend it against his opponent."[20] In laymen's terms, a stronghold is a mindset or thought process. Could it be that many of the things we so adamantly blame on the devil are in fact really caused by our thought process and mindsets? For example, the enemy has not sent an attack on your finance if the truth is that you lack basic understanding of key financial principles by which you should govern your spending and saving. If you are in the third generation in your family on public assistance, with no education or plan to gain education, poverty is not a spirit that needs to be cast out of you. It is a mindset that has developed in your family unit that has to be investigated and terminated.

The frontline of defense in the battle of spiritual warfare is dealing with the battle for your underlying thought process. Most of the situations and circumstances we find ourselves in are not due to a cosmic conspiracy to destroy us. A great majority of our negative life dilemmas came from an incorrect thought pattern that led us to the point we are at right now. The honest truth is that most of the Body of Christ has incorrect thinking in regards to major life scenarios, and this gives legal access to the enemy to come in through technicalities of wrong thinking.

Spiritual warfare must begin to happen not just in our moments of contemplative prayer, or even through prophetic declarations and extended periods of fasting, but it must happen through the upgrading of our thought processes and the pulling down of old mindsets. Drug addicts often have the ability to shake the chemical dependency and physical function of addiction. However if the stronghold or pattern of thought that led them into the destructive behavior in the first place is not completely shattered, then relapse in inevitable. The same is true of any person, no matter what the particulars of their proclivity are. Their minds must be submitted to the will, way, and Law of God in order for them to see victory in their lives.

Moment of Clarity: How much of your present life panorama is a result of a thought process completely askew from your personal goals and aspirations? What strongholds have been controlling your life that you have allowed to rob you of your victory and testimony? In what area will you break out of a pattern of thought that is not even your own? My prayer for you is that the God of all Heaven and earth will reveal to you the strongholds in your life that allow the enemy access to your wealth, health, and overall well-being.

Chapter 14
Breaking the Bondage of the Mind

Reasonings bringing down, and every high thing lifted up against the knowledge of God, and bringing into captivity every thought to the obedience of the Christ,[21]
2 Corinthians 10:5

In the last chapter we looked at the concept of strongholds and what they truly are. However, merely identifying what a stronghold is does not empower an individual to have victory over it. Understanding that a stronghold is an overarching mindset or system of thought, the way to change a mindset is to deal with each thought on a one-on-one basis. So in 2 Corinthians 10:5, we are instructed not to bring an entire mindset under submission to the counterculture of the Kingdom, but to submit each individual thought to the obedience of Christ.

The mindset of the Kingdom is determined by the mandates of the King. A mandate is "an authoritative command; especially: a formal order from a superior court or official to an inferior one an authorization to act given to a representative."[22] These mandates are given to us in the Word of God and are specified "for teaching, for conviction, for setting aright, for instruction that is in righteousness, that the man of God may be fitted—for every good work having been completed."[23] As we submit to the mandates of the Word of God, we are made whole and complete through the renewing of our mindsets.

Mandates then are designed to be the seeds of mindsets. The strongholds that keep you trapped in destructive patters are easily replaced by thoughts that fuel success and genius, when those mandates of the Kingdom are activated. When you appropriate these mandates to your heart, they become a mindset and ultimately a culture.

Metacognition is a prerequisite for Kingdom culture, which is the culture of success. Without processing the mandates to the point that you allow them to become mindsets, you will never fully be initiated into the culture of excellence that belongs to every Kingdom citizen. There is much work in submitting your every thought to the light of the Word of God, and I will not pretend it is an easy task. The things we take as commonplace can be totally contrary to the truth of the Word, and resigning yourself to be in line with what is often uncomfortable is most frequently a process of pensive contrition.

Moment of Clarity: How much of what you thought today was really in accordance with the mandates of God? How many mandates did you follow because they have become your mindset, or was your obedience fear based? How much of your thought process has been replaced by the vista of the Kingdom? When we really begin to evaluate ourselves in the Light of the glorious Gospel of Jesus Christ, we find that our thought processes and mindsets are subpar to His Excellency and greatness. My prayer for you is that as you have identified the strongholds in your life that are contrary to the mindset of the Kingdom, you will repent and embrace what is greater for your life.

Chapter 15
Power of the Mind!

Commit your works to the Lord, And your thoughts will be established.[24]
Proverbs 16:3

Everyone wants to be prosperous. Whether you are from Prague or Zimbabwe, we are part of a generation seeking fulfillment with prosperity. It is no longer acceptable to work jobs that have no meaning and to sell your life to a company that has no loyalty to you, in order to pay for a boat or car that you have no time to enjoy. This is a generation where people are choosing jobs that give their life meaning. They are partnering and networking to make their income match their output in a marketplace dance that leaves people outside of this bandwidth wondering if their sons and daughters will ever find stability and settle down to a "real job". The sad reality is that while economists and social exegetes report this as the common scenario, many people in this generation are in hot pursuit of this fulfillment and balance, only to find that this brass ring is easier to see than to catch. Hot pursuit soon leads to disenchantment, and a general discontent, causing many to opt out altogether and to settle into a life of mediocrity that appeases people for whom they have already lost respect.

Solomon, who was said to have been the wisest man ever to live at the height of his success, recorded for us words of wisdom that speak directly to where we are as a global village. He tells us, in his narrative on wisdom, to commit our works unto the Lord and our thoughts will be established. One translator put it this way: "Roll unto Jehovah thy works, And established are thy purposes,"[25] The wisdom is this—when you make God the center of your endeavors, the things you think about accomplishing for Him come into manifestation.

Perhaps you are currently frustrated that some of your thoughts still hang in dream form, waiting to be brought into the earth realm, but you have not considered that the dreams and thoughts you have are of little or no effect in the Kingdom of God. The work you are trying to accomplish is to build an empire or kingdom to yourself, so it is not necessary for manifestation to come to fruition in your life. A change in the direction of the focus of your work would provide the needed spiritual motility to catapult your thinking to the next level and to pull manifestation from the seed of your thoughts. As believers, we are constrained to be on assignment from our Commander in Chief, and our thoughts must be dedicated to His best interest and not our own. We are in the employ of His service, and our whole selves are given with singleness of thought to advancing His Kingdom.

Moment of Clarity: In this purpose-driven world, most of us do not stop to think what is driving our purposes. My thoughts have value, but what are the values of my thoughts? Take some time to search the purpose of your thoughts. Find your core values and see if your thought process lines up with the agenda of the Kingdom. Ask yourself if your thoughts are valuable outside of you. My prayer for you is that all of your thoughts will come to manifestation as they line up with the agenda of the Heavens, and that your greatness will be unlocked by the power of your purpose in God!

Chapter 16
What Am I Thinking?

As to the rest, brethren, as many things as are true, as many as are grave, as many as are righteous, as many as are pure, as many as are lovely, as many as are of good report, if any worthiness, and if any praise, these things think upon…[26]
Philippians 4:8

If the average person took a poll of his or her positive thoughts in a day, and his or her negative thoughts in the same day, which category do you believe would outweigh the other? Now consider the last twenty four hours of your own life and ask yourself which category would be full. The natural propensity of human nature is to have a bent toward the negative. Most of us would do well to take a hard look at our own balance between healthy productive thoughts and thoughts that sap our energy by wasting our focus on things that we can never change.

Paul writes to the Philippian church from a Roman prison his most fatherly of all epistles. With a warm and compassionate heart, he writes to a group of people he loves dearly on various topics that will be of benefit to them while he is away from them. As he draws this letter to a close, he ends on a note which the King James Version translates "Finally my brethren". The whole of his writing leads them not to a commandment about conduct or even about character, but about their own thought process. Once again there is a clarion call to active metacognition, which Paul later promises will lead to "the God of peace." A phrase known to a Jewish mind as a very name of God could not be missed by any of the readers to whom the author originally addressed. It appears that he gives them prerequisites for thoughts that will lead to their seeing God manifest Himself as peace in their lives.

We understand that as Paul penned these words to this congregation, the Spirit of God was breathing these words out through him for us! Peace in our lives comes from thoughts that center on the very concepts Paul introduced to this church over two thousand years ago. Have you ever stopped to think that perhaps your life progress has been impeded not by a lack of hard work and dedication but by a lack of the right thoughts? Has negativity been your companion for so long that it has robbed you of a fresh perspective for advancement? Paul gives a clear blueprint for the criteria of successful thinking. We would do well to place our thoughts next to this paradigm to discover whether or not we qualify for success.

Moment of Clarity: As I interface with leaders across the nation, I can always distinguish seasoned success from new attempts at leadership. Those who are seasoned can see what went right in a situation, and those still attempting can tell me only what went wrong. If you really want to see peace manifest in your life, spend one whole day rejecting any thought that does not line up with Paul's prescription for right thinking. See if you can focus on positive aspects and dimensions to old situations and/or problems you may be facing, and you will be amazed at the depth of your own creativity. My prayer for you is that your vista will shift to your being a solution-focused problem solver, and that the Lord will grant you insight into what is right, and grace for what is wrong.

Chapter 17
Think Your Way to Purpose

The thoughts of the righteous are right: but the counsels of the wicked are deceit.[27]
Proverbs 12:5

In the original language, the word for "thoughts" in this text is *machashabah,* and it means "plan, purpose, or invention." Purpose is never realized without thought in the form of plans. Have you ever stopped to consider whether or not your thoughts or plans are right? If we are to call ourselves righteous, then that which we think about and focus our attention and concentration on must be right, but most of us have no measurement of what right is. The word *mishpat* is an interesting word study which means "judgment, justice, or ordinance." It even means "the act of deciding a case or process, procedure, litigation (before judges)." There is a connotation in the word of executing orders.[28]

This is very interesting because when most people analyze their plans and thoughts, they find that those thoughts are not focused on the execution of the judgments of God and are not in line with His ordinances. Somehow we have gotten away from thinking thoughts that are Godly directive and have begun to set our humanistic thinking up before God, as if He is responsible to acknowledge our thoughts instead of us surrendering to His. The propensity of the majority of people I meet is to decide what they want to do and to ask God to bless it, rather than purposing in their hearts to accomplish what He has blessed.

I very much wanted to work in the entertainment industry, in music management. I knew this was not the will of God for my life; however, I desperately wanted to pursue that career. I thought that I could please God by making a compromise. I would work in music management in the Christian music industry, since I knew my life would be dedicated to

Kingdom advancement. I enrolled in school and prayed that the Lord would bless me to graduate and find employment. I made a deal with God and told Him if He would let me pursue this, I would serve Him the rest of my life. I knew in my spirit that He agreed. I finished school and graduated, but I have never officially worked one day in the area of that degree. The day I graduated, it was as if I heard God say "My turn," and my whole world changed. My thoughts were not the thoughts of the Kingdom. They were self-centered and misguided at best.

As soon as I began to focus on the things that He had planned for my life, everything shifted and came into place. No matter how I tried and applied for a position in my field, I could not get into that door. Now, doors swing open for me on a consistent basis since I have turned my thoughts in the direction of complete submission to Kingdom advancement. The happiness I searched for in doing and thinking according to my own system escaped me, but in thinking the thoughts that originate in God, I have found total fulfillment.

Moment of Clarity: How much of your thought process is right? How much of your planning involves actively taking into consideration the will and precepts of God? Let me ask you to consider whether or not the way you have been thinking and planning has worked well for you in the past. Does your fruitfulness show that the thoughts of your life are the plans of God? Take a moment to search your heart for the truth as it relates to what agenda your plans are really on. My prayer for you is that your plans will be right. Righteousness in the thought process establishes a paradigm for how your manifestation will function. It is my prayer that your thoughts will line up with the prescription of good works designed for your life.

Chapter 18
Guard Your Thoughts

Beware lest there be a wicked thought in your heart, saying, 'The seventh year, the year of release, is at hand, 'and your eye be evil against your poor brother and you give him nothing, and he cry out to the Lord against you, and it become sin among you.

Deuteronomy 15:9

As Moses explains God's law concerning the year of release to the children of Israel, he lays out a plan for the restoration of all things. Knowing that this system of debt relief goes against the sinful human nature of all people, and that greed would cause some to instantly rebel; he issues this warning to all of Israel. The words must have stung as they stood to hear the law, "Beware lest there be a wicked thought!" Imagine that as our Heavenly Father gives you instructions on righteous living or the plans that He has concerning your life, He is standing before you with the same warning to beware of wicked thoughts.

Our thoughts are the seeds of our deeds. Everything that is created is created twice, first in the mind and second in the tangible realm. All of the evil deeds ever committed by you or anyone else were first in seed form as thought, no matter how brief the thought may have been. Even if only for a split second before you committed an offence, there was a transmittal point from thought to action. With this framework in mind, a warning system is so needful for our success in Christ. If we guard our thoughts from wickedness, we will be able to protect our actions from sin.

The word wicked carries many connotations for each of us. In Deuteronomy 15:9, the word "wicked" is *bâliya'al* and it means "worthless, good for nothing, unprofitable, or base fellow."[29] So the idea in the text of a wicked thought is one that is worthless or unprofitable. These are the thoughts that lead to ungodly behavior. Stop for a moment to think of how many thoughts you entertained today that were actually what God calls wicked! Our days are often filled with idle thoughts that lead to zero productivity, but as believers we are called to fruitful multiplication. Your call as a follower of Christ is to set your thoughts towards redemptive productivity and to repent of wicked thoughts.

Moment of Clarity: There is one less day on the calendar of your life. How did you spend it? If you are unsatisfied with the quality of the life you live, it may well be that you should examine whether or not your thoughts are wicked. How much of your day is given over to thoughts that have no potential for producing the life that you desire to lead? Where will your dreams gain their fuel? Today, check your thoughts by your conversation: how much of your speech has depth and meaning and how much of it is idle banter, leading to no productivity? My prayer for you is that your mind will be filled with all the grace of God and that each thought will be one of great value.

Chapter 19
Life Lesson

The hardest thing about preaching and pastoring people is not dealing with people. It is dealing with yourself. There is a demand on you not only to be truthful with the Scripture that you preach from, but also to be truthful with yourself about who you really are and where you are in your heart. Real ministry has more to do with managing yourself and helping others to manage themselves, and less to do with pulpit preaching. Coming to that understanding has been key in whatever personal success I have achieved.

In order to walk in honesty, I am continually monitoring my thought process to see if there is anything that would hinder the preaching of the Gospel or my leadership from being pleasing to God. I am not monitoring for perfection, but rather, I look for all the opportunities to improve on anything that might get in the way of Kingdom success. On a personal note, the awareness of metacognition has greatly changed the way I view my own leadership. The Word has come alive to me in a new way, in that even when preaching or counseling someone, I am more prone to think in terms of why I say or do what I am saying or doing.

My challenge as a leader is, when I discover the thought process behind my own thoughts, what do I do about it? As we have thus far examined the power and essence of thought, we have to look at whether or not we will be willing to change the pattern of our thoughts to achieve excellence in our lives. As we look further into the shaping of our lives through thoughts at this juncture, we have to consider our commitment to right thinking.

Moment of Clarity: How important is your personal growth and development? What are you willing to change internally to gain access to the thoughts that will propel you toward destiny? The systems of your life have been built on the foundation of your thought process to this point, so how many of your systems are you willing to give up if they do not line up with a thought process that is beneficial to your destiny? My prayer for you is that God will give your heart the courage to face your own fears and also the strength to confront your own thought process.

Chapter 20
The Aroma of Genius

Now thanks be to God who always leads us in triumph in Christ, and through us diffuses the fragrance of His knowledge in every place.

2 Corinthians 2:14

In this passage of sacred text, the Apostle Paul writes to the church of Corinth about restoration and reconciliation, but he sneaks in a secret formula for victory. Here in this letter, proclaiming his love for a very fickle group of people who are not sure of his true spiritual authority or his rightful place in the Kingdom, Paul pauses to give away a Kingdom mystery that is overlooked by most of us as we read the text. Here is the mystery: thank God for leading you to victory through knowledge!

"Knowledge" in this text is the word *gnosis*, which signifies in general "intelligence and understanding." Coupled with that understanding, the word carries with it the general connotation of "knowledge of Christian religion." In fact, it is "the deeper, more perfect and enlarged knowledge of this religion, such as belongs to the more advanced, esp. of things lawful and unlawful for Christians."[30] This is the knowledge that brings about victory in our lives. Paul's idea of the Church and/or Christianity was not about feeling like a good and moral person, but it was about experiencing victory in your life through the thought process of the Kingdom. There is much to be said about learning general knowledge. Contrary to popular opinion knowing things other than Bible verses does not take away from your relationship with Christ, but rather enhances it when the knowledge is coupled with an understanding of divine things. The more you grow in the things of Christ, the more you understand the light that the Word sheds on every facet of your existence, and you become better for having the knowledge.

Triumph in your life stems from a deep knowledge of the systems of God. In the book of Daniel, he and his three friends found themselves in Babylonian captivity working in the king's palace because they were skillful in all knowledge and able to understand science. They had an aptitude for language, which shows a measure of mental dexterity. The Bible says that because Daniel and his friends implemented the system of God, they were found to be ten times better than those who where training with them. Soon they were all elevated in the palace to become high-ranking government officials.

Moment of Clarity: Kingdom thinkers are always ahead of the curve and they continually come out on top. There is a certain standard that Kingdom knowledge brings to the table in the marketplace that elevates those who partake in it. Do you separate your sacred and secular thought process or have you integrated your world? Keeping your life separate is a grave mistake because your Kingdom genius is needed in the center of daily activities. Ask yourself if you have given yourself to a system of thought that integrates both sacred and secular thoughts into one Kingdom advancing paradigm. Your triumph is in your ability to release the fragrance of His knowledge in the earth. My prayer for you is that God will give you opportunity to release His knowledge into your sphere of influence today, that your life will be full of integrated thought which situates you in high places before great men, and finally that the God of all knowledge will grant you His attentions as you reach for triumph in every area of your life.

Chapter 21
It Can't Be Bought!

But Peter said to him, "Your money perish with you, because you thought that the gift of God could be purchased with money!
Acts 8:20

Here again we find a new Greek word that gives us insight into our thoughts. The word in this text is *nomizo*, which means "a custom, or the received usage; to hold by custom or usage, own as a custom or usage; to follow a custom or usage."[31] In other words, this thought process that Peter speaks of consists of thoughts that cause us to process information through customs. In each of our families, there are cultural norms or customs by which we function and live together in harmony or discord. What causes discord is when one violates the customs that are accepted and agreed upon.

When we do not violate the culture or customs that have been set forth by the King, it keeps peace in the Kingdom. This task is very much an undertaking because most of our thought processes have been programmed by a different system of thought. Being born into sin via the nature of all humanity, we are accustomed to the norms and mores of the kingdom of darkness. Our thoughts are then instinctively programmed to be contrary to the mindset of Godliness. The better acquainted we are with the nuances of sin and its customs, the more difficult it is to process anything through any other system. The culture dominates our thinking and becomes the backdrop for all of our decisions.

This wrong thinking becomes to us a curse according to Acts 8:20, because it causes us to devalue what is in the Kingdom of Light. Things that have great worth and value in the Kingdom are completely misjudged by those who operate on a system of darkness. Those who seek to add to their life via the vehicle of tangible goods will be greatly disappointed to find out that goods can only fill a small portion of their life void. Things like righteousness, peace, and joy cannot be bought or sold on the open market, and the value of these things cannot be measured monetarily. In fact, while the currency of the kingdom of darkness is finance, the currency of the Kingdom of God is faith, and there is a foundational difference in people who operate under the currency of each kingdom. While faith can produce finance, finance cannot produce faith. Faith may be strengthened by a manifestation of finance, but it cannot be made by finance. The curse of old custom thinking is that it locks you in to what that custom can produce.

Moment of Clarity: What cultural and customary thought processes are producing curses in your life? Ask yourself, what are the motivating factors that contribute to your view on a particular matter? Have you thought about the customs in your life that keep you from fully embracing the Kingdom? There is so much in our everyday lives that we can attribute to custom; from the time we wake up to the time we go to bed, we are constantly interfacing with culture, and yet we spend very little time considering the culture which we base our view of life on. My prayer for you is that God will grant you the spirit of revelation that will cause you to see with clarity the customs that are governing your life, and that you will know His heart and culture.

Chapter 22
It's Not Always What It Looks Like

Now Hannah spoke in her heart; only her lips moved, but her voice was not heard. Therefore Eli thought she was drunk.[32]
I Samuel 1:13

Even the most devote and austere of men can have the wrong thought because his eyes deceive him. When Eli happened upon Hannah praying to God, he thought she was drunk because her lips were moving and yet no sounds came out. He did not know of the pain this parishioner lived in at home. She loved her husband and he loved her, and yet no matter how they came together for intimate moments, she could not conceive. There was no wrongdoing or sin on either part. The text simply lets us know that the Lord, in His own sovereignty, had shut up her womb. To make matters worse, as it was the custom of that day, her husband had another wife and she was able to conceive just fine. It seems that this wife took the role of an antagonist and taunted Hannah about the fact that she had no children to show as a manifestation of her relationship and connection to the husband she shared with another wife. Hannah had no one to take care of her should something happen to her husband.

In this state of distress and anguish Hannah found herself alone at the altar in the house of God, frustrated with unfulfilled purpose. She had all of the faculties to produce, and yet productivity escaped her. Nothing seemed to be going right and she was at a point of desperation, when in walked Eli. He was the priest and a prophet of God; surely he would see and discern that she was trying desperately to make contact with God to get an answer for her crisis. However, instead of seeing the cry for help and a plea for relief, Eli determines, based on evidence that is misinterpreted, that this women in need is nothing more than a drunk.

How many times have we misread the evidence and fixed it in our minds that something was one way, only to learn later that it was exactly the opposite? The thing about thoughts is that they are often developed when evidence is evaluated, and sometimes the evidence is misjudged. I am persuaded that a great number of relationships have ended based on false evidence appearing to be real, and the unfortunate thing is that after the truth is discovered, the damage is too great to heal. It is imperative that we guard our thoughts from the distraction of false evidence, and that we continually walk in the light of the truth.

Moment of Clarity: How much of what you think regarding the circumstances of your life is based on false evidence? Do you consider the fact that perception is a big part of how you relate to and interact with people around you? Are you cognizant of the enemy's strategy to keep you from embracing your Kingdom destiny by presenting you with distorted pictures of truth? Maybe you should take a moment to evaluate things currently facing you and determine if you are walking in the light. My prayer for you is that God will grant you clarity of vision, that your thoughts may be informed by Kingdom truths and not by false evaluations.

Chapter 23
Think Yourself Prosperous

The thoughts of the diligent tend only to plenteousness; but of every one that is hasty only to want.[33]
Proverbs 21:5

The only way to real prosperity is through the door of purpose. Distraction comes through the door of divergent thoughts. In the world of advertising, the United Negro College Fund had one of the most successful ad campaigns of its time. The slogan was "A mind is a terrible thing to waste." How true this is when our thoughts are not directed to our purpose.

In Proverbs 21: 5, Solomon uses the word *mowthar* which translates "preeminence, abundance, profit, or superiority; to describe plenteousness." It is a Biblical concept that the direction of your thoughts determines in your profitability and abundance. In this hour in the history of the Church, there are continual messages preached from pulpits across the world that there is a Kingdom wealth transfer about to come to the Body of Christ. I personally believe the message is accurate, but I believe most of us lack the tools necessary to qualify for the wealth when it comes to the Church. In order to access and maintain the abundance of God and the wealth that accompanies it, our thoughts must tend only to plenteousness.

If you have an honest assessment of your own thought process, you may discover that there is some polarity in your direction when it comes to your own success. Some of this division of thought may come from situations or circumstances that have clouded your vision. I have found for many people that the source of this division is that they have not found examples or paradigms to hold up as a blueprint for achieving the end goal. One of the most powerful tools I have discovered in keeping my mind on the purpose of God in my life is the tool of surrounding myself with people who have like thought processes. You will never be able to establish a brand of excellence if you continually surround yourself with people who think on a generic level.

Proverbs 21: 5 addresses people with a want or lack mentality, and there is no praise for this thought process. To surround yourself or to even connect yourself to these people, you will begin to develop thought patterns and processes that lead you to the same destination of purpose and destiny. I have a rule when connecting with people: I first have to know where they see themselves in five years, and then where they see me in five years. The answer to these two questions determines how close they can be to me, because in order to qualify for where God is taking me, I have to maintain thoughts of prosperity and purpose.

Moment of Clarity: Of all the people in your life, how many would you consider to be people of purpose verses those who are hasty? How many of your connections are headed in the Kingdom direction that leads to prosperity with a purpose? How much more could you accomplish if the models of prosperity you know are yours through Christ, were tangible in your life? I am concerned that this is a generation of people whose thoughts are divided because there is no paradigm for them to pattern themselves after. My prayer for you is that you will discover the thoughts that lead to your success. I pray that the Lord will increase and decrease your circle until it includes those whose hearts are fixed on His glory.

Chapter 24
Planning for Purpose

Every purpose is established by counsel: and with good advice make war.[34]
Proverbs 20:18

We dealt earlier with the word for purpose, *machashabah*, which connotes a thought in the form of a plan. This wisdom of Solomon speaks of your thoughts being informed by good counsel. Much of our planning and purposing in our hearts comes as a result of our giftedness and personality. Because of this, we fail many times to see pitfalls associated with our own genius. They are built in blind spots designed for us to live lives of interdependence. We are not made to be isolated; rather, we are designed to be in fellowship with the Almighty God and one another.

Counsel provides for us a safety net that keeps us from running headlong into traps set by the enemy to thwart our destiny and progress. Many great plans have come to naught because of a built-in fault line that no one was close enough to the architect of the plan to point out. Recently, we have seen a rash of major ministries tumble, crash, and even burn because of pride and alienation. There is often no real heart-connecting and submission to counselors who can help individuals navigate the obstacle course that will hinder the success of the plan of God. Also, there is often no true submitting of our thoughts for input from trusted leaders who have a proven track record of Kingdom success.

Sometimes our thoughts are motivated by our egos and sometimes they are even generated from the underworld. Counsel allows us to filter our thoughts through a spiritual sieve to strain out any impurities that might be caught in the fabric of our thought process. I personally function in the office of an Apostle, a high office in the Lord's Church, but I am spiritually connected to an Apostolic Council of Elders who I can bounce ideas and thoughts off of before moving hastily ahead in any one direction. It is for me a measure of wisdom that I know has and will serve me well in my pursuit of the Kingdom.

Moment of Clarity: Everyone needs someone who understands their Kingdom destiny, who they can present their thoughts to for review and input. Do you have a person or persons to whom you hold your thoughts and plans accountable? Consider Paul and Barnabus and their ministry to the Gentiles. As the ministry began to grow, they sought the input of the other apostles and brethren. Acts the fifteenth chapter records the story of the Jerusalem Council, where the apostles came together for the examination of the plans for the Gentiles. If these great men of God could submit to counsel, why is it that we find it so difficult today? My prayer for you is that God will strategically place people in your life who will serve as safe counsel for the plans He has put in you, and that you will fight the temptation of pride that would cause you to hold your thoughts and plans so close that no one could point out the danger zones. I pray that the advice you will receive will be directly from the throne room of God in all things.

Chapter 25
Government of the Mind, an Essay

Making a commitment to right thinking is sometimes the hardest part of metacognition. The idea of monitoring your thoughts and living by a standard of right thinking is not appealing to the average individual. As I interact on a daily basis with this postmodern generation, I realize more that this generation is most comfortable going with what works for the moment, living not by a set of mandates but rather by an emotion-based life of what brings momentary pleasure.

The drug crisis and the AIDS pandemic can partly be pinned on a mindset that does not think in terms of goals or consequences. It is the direct link to people making choices based on temporary comfort over long term success. Most of what we are facing now is a lack of overarching principles that govern the thought process of a generation that links beliefs to behavior.

Never before have we seen a generation that claims to be spiritual, but lacks morality. There is no connection between what is viewed as spiritual and what is lived out on a functional daily level and that presents to us a problem with the Church. The Church has lost its platform in the marketplace because there are no clear, set rules of engagement which govern our thoughts, and thereby govern our behavior. A recipe for disaster is found in a life without lines or boundaries.

Moment of Clarity: We must begin to dialog with everyone in our circle of influence on the topic of metacognition. It is this process that will allow us to guard ourselves from wilderness wandering. Have you taken the time to give your thoughts the attention necessary to arm them with the tools they need to produce the greatness that is inside of you? I am fully convinced that we must call this generation back into a focus of thought. When you begin to develop a systematic thought process, it brings your life into focus. My prayer for you is that through the power of the Word you will discover guiding principles that will activate right thought in your life; that God will grant you all knowledge of the Kingdom through encounters with His presence and moments with His Law.

Chapter 26
Blessed Thinking

Blessed is the man that walketh not in the counsel of the ungodly, nor standeth in the way of sinners, nor sitteth in the seat of the scornful. But his delight is in the law of the LORD*; and in his law doth he meditate day and night.*
Psalm 1:1

There is a blessing assigned to thinking about the Word of God that cannot be ignored. The blessing is so powerful that this passage of Scripture goes on to say that whatever this person does will prosper when the thoughts of the Word are combined with the actions and attitudes described therein. What a wonderful promise given to us, that what is inside the Word of God contains what we need to be successful in our every endeavor, if only the Word becomes the fuel of our thoughts.

As I browse through the business sections and self-help sections of the neighborhood bookstore that I frequent, I cannot help but to notice the multiplicity of titles and authors who all contradict one another in their introductions alone. I am puzzled at how people come to a decision on whose advice they should adhere to on any one topic. I often think how confusing it must be to begin searching out a topic new to you if there is no particular guide or mentor to help focus your research. With the addition of the millions of entries available via the Internet, whose validity you cannot even trace to a specific author, you enter into a state of total frenzy.

This first verse in the book of Psalm sets the Bible apart from all other books in that it claims to produce knowledge on every level and subject that is totally fail-proof. There is hidden within the text a powerful concept, and that is meditation on the Word of God will unlock ultimate success in your life. The word for "meditate" in this text is *hagah*, which literally means "to meditate, devise, muse, or imagine." Therein lies the secret of managing your thoughts: they must be grounded in a knowledge of the Word of God. This is basic, yet so major, and the average Christian misses the light when it comes to our thoughts by using outside influences to evaluate whether or not he or she is on track.

The time spent in the Word is the most valuable investment you can make with your day. The Word becomes the fuel that energizes the mobility of your life. Once you determine to live according to the principles of the Word of God, it is safe to trust yourself completely to Him. There is nothing more important that you can do to enhance your world and to better your life than to mature your thought process through the Word of God. Many men of modern times have found success through Biblical principles even when they have not found salvation, because the Law of the Lord is perfect.

Moment of Clarity: When thinking about the value of the Word of God, one must know that your level of success is in direct proportion to your knowledge of the Word. Governing your thoughts by the Law of God is not optional for those who want to produce fruit that will endure. Leaving a legacy and inheritance for your children will manifest by understanding Kingdom principles for wealth and wisdom found in the Word of God. My father taught me that the Word of God is the final court of arbitration in the life of the believer, and these are words I have lived by that help govern my thoughts and behavior. Ask yourself; "How much of the story of God have I deposited in my spirit?" My prayer for you is that you will increase in all the knowledge of the Word of God. I pray that your heart will be saturated with the imprint of God's signature through the power of the revelation of His Word.

Chapter 27
A Thoughtful Heart

For out of the heart come forth evil thoughts, murders, adulteries, whoredoms, thefts, false witnessings, evil speakings: these are the things defiling the man; but to eat with unwashen hands doth not defile the man.[35]

Matthew 15:19

To make common (Levitically) unclean, or defile, to make profane and to declare or count unclean[36]; this is *koinoo*, and it is the word in the text used to speak of defiling a man. All the things that are contrary to success and living in a season of prosperity are the result of the thoughts of your heart. In this text, Christ is making the point that the thoughts of a man produce the behaviors that denote failure. There is a direct link, according to Christ's teaching, between the thoughts of your heart and the quality of life you live.

After taking the time to walk this far in this book, you should be really acquainted with your own thoughts and should be working on understanding why you think the way you do. I am acutely aware that change always has its challenges, and so by now you may well be asking yourself if the process is worth it. This is my pause to remind you that everything in your future is riding on your ability to change your own cognition! Whatever your life map looks like to this point is a result of your thoughts and in order to change the picture you see into the picture you want to see, you have to change your thoughts.

What Christ calls evil thoughts are summed up in the word chosen by the author, which is *dialogismos*: "the thinking of a man deliberating with himself; a thought or inward reasoning; a deliberating, questioning about what is true; any hesitation, doubting, disputing, and/or arguing" is all found in the definition of the word.[37] These are the thoughts that Christ calls evil—doubting yourself, vision, dream, or call. How long will you wrestle with changing your mindset to be like Christ's?

For many years I wrestled with the call of God on my life. It was something that did not sound good or pleasant to my own plans and desires. I did not mind working in the church or serving God in some capacity, but giving my life totally to the work of the Lord was not the most exciting concept. The worst part of the wrestling was the total dissatisfaction with everything and everyone else. No matter where I went or tried, there was a pull to the grace of God and a spirit of excellence that I could not put my finger on, but I could not see it anywhere I turned. So I wrestled with saying yes to God, but the peace I searched for never came until I surrendered to a new concept of who I really am. When I really embraced the heart of God for my life, it became a picture of His purpose for me.

Moment of Clarity: What are you holding back in your own life by struggling unnecessarily with the mind of God for you? Are you still debating about whether or not your mindset needs to shift? Ask yourself, what do you have to lose by submitting to the power of the Word? Your next dimension of life is not being held up by an outside entity or force; there is nothing holding back the promise of God over your life greater than your own willingness to surrender your thought process to the mind of Christ. If your thoughts have been evil, then my prayer for you is that this journey to change thought process becomes a life journey. It is my prayer that you will stay continually in the pursuit of learning the height and depth of the riches of Christ Jesus!

Chapter 28
Stop Thinking?

And he said unto his disciples, Therefore I say unto you, Take no thought for your life, what ye shall eat; neither for the body, what ye shall put on.[38]
Luke 12:22

Stress has become a major focus of life in the 21st century. There are a myriad of authors and self-help gurus whose sole professional concentration is centered on helping people eliminate stress. Much of the world is overworked and underpaid. In nations like India, American companies have outsourced jobs and changed the makeup of the cultural infrastructure of whole people groups. Night jobs for single mothers and downsizing across the board are all factors that contribute to the instability of the home resulting in unilateral stress. Whether the family has one or two people working, the marketplace overflows with stressed out individuals in need of relief.

More and more, as people join themselves to our local church, I find myself sitting face to face with Christians who are overcome by stress. Many coming to us from other ministries where they have been victims of church hurt, or those coming with deep family wounds and emotional scarring, all seem to manifest visible signs of stress. This all causes me to wonder why as Bible believing, redeemed Saints of the Most High God, the effects of this day to day stress seem to be taking as large a toll on us as it is on those who operate in the kingdom of darkness. I wonder if there is some fundamental flaw in our approach to Christianity, or is our general approach to life causing us to be stretched to maximum capacity?

After wrestling with many hypotheses as I was listening for the Spirit of the Lord, He directed me to this passage. Everything came swiftly into focus as the illumination of His Word flooded my soul! Take no thought! The answer had been here all the time; we have been stressed because we have used our mental faculties for things they were never designed to focus on. In the Greek, *merimnao* expresses the concept "to be troubled with cares." It literally means "to seek to promote one's interests."[39] There it is plain as day: we are stressed out because all of our mind power is focused on the care of our own needs. It is not just that the focus of our thoughts is on our daily provision, but, the concept is that the focus of our thoughts is to worry about our needs.

In every great relationship there is a law in action called the law of reciprocation. Reciprocal relations mean that as I am blessed, I am blessing you also. In a good marriage, the job of the husband is to focus on pleasing and loving the wife, while the job of the wife is pleasing and loving the husband. What will not work long term if both people are focused on pleasing only one person. Eventually, someone recognizes that no one is taking care of him or her, and trouble will shortly ensue. This law is true as we consider our relationship with our sovereign King. If we think only to focus on our own need, we will abandon our quest to please Him. How then can He be free to meet our needs unless we seek only His will?

We face stress on a daily basis mostly because we have allowed worry to be the dominant thought process that governs not only our internal factors, but our external responses as well. The command to "take no thought for your life" comes not as a license to living in reckless abandon, but it comes as a warning against the danger of unnecessary worry. If we have the assurance that our Heavenly Father is a kind and benevolent King, we must ask ourselves why we doubt His goodness.

Moment of Clarity: There are many outside stimuli that would cause moments of stress, but your internal thought process is under your control. How you respond to circumstance and situation is predicated on whether or not your cognition tells you that Christ is the answer in every crisis. We do not live without hope, because of the fact that we are in covenant relationship with the Hope of Glory; therefore, our minds should be free to concentrate on the good things of God, knowing that He is the author and finisher of our faith. If I believe that God will take care of my life then my mind is free to focus on getting from here to there. Ask yourself if you are trapped by anxious thinking. Are you losing a grip on the promises of God because you have lost sight of Jesus as your help? My prayer for you today is that you will be challenged to radical faith, and that your mind will be free from worry. I pray that God will grant you Divine peace. I pray that you will be so consumed with accomplishing much for Christ that there is no time for doubt. May the arm of the Lord be mighty in you!

Chapter 29
A Wisdom Download

And if any of you do lack wisdom, let him ask from God, who is giving to all liberally, and not reproaching, and it shall be given to him…[40]
James 1:5

After finally understanding the need to submit to the lifelong process of active metacognition and being empowered with the tool by which to analyze your thoughts, I understand that for many of us there is the question, "Where do I personally begin the journey after I have concluded this book?" The answer may be much more simplistic than one would think. In fact, the answer can be summed up in two words: ask God.

Our thoughts must be generated not by what we have come to understand through the process of growing up and developing, but rather, they must come from the heart of God Himself. He must be the one and only progenitor of our new system of thinking. God alone sits at the end of all things with an eye towards the beginning, with the power to call all things after the counsel of His own will. His ways and thoughts are higher than ours, so high that they are as far from us as the heavens themselves, and yet He rules in the kingdoms of men and gives them to whomever He chooses. The knowledge of God is older than antiquity and vaster than the expanse of all the distant galaxies combined. He alone has the power to infuse your spirit with God thought!

To ask or *aiteo* is "to beg, call for, crave, desire, or require." This is a strong word in that it indicates that one must approach God with a depth of passion that shows a desperation for His wisdom. Your thoughts will never change until they are exchanged for the wisdom of God. The wisdom of God is released by your desperation for it. Wisdom in the Old Testament is depicted as a "she," longing to be desired, pursued, chased, wanted, and needed. If you are to embrace her, you must woo her. Your need for more knowledge must become your passion, and even your thirst.

You cannot get what you need to bring yourself into the place of mental maturity without a release from God. Just a quick glance at James 1: 5 will not produce what you need; it is in moments in His presence where His face turns towards you. The favor of the Lord must come into your life to cause you to arrive in places of Divine connections and at pivotal moments of destiny that are preordained to lead you to your success.

Moment of Clarity: Without God we are nothing. I have a church mother who continues to remind us that the word of life is, "It is all about God." Changing your thought process must have as its ultimate end the glory of God. By no means can you begin to tap the unsearchable riches of His glory with an eye single to your own betterment. Because the glory of God is the ultimate end of man, we must approach Him in fear and reverence as we submit ourselves to seek His face for a release of wisdom that will transform our knowledge and create the platform for our success. All the while, we know that our success is not ours but the glory goes to Jesus. No one else is a factor in our worship or adoration when we know that everything we have comes from Him and it is to Him we owe all things. My prayer for you is that you will ask God not for success or fortune, but rather that you will beg Him for wisdom.

Chapter 30
GO!

Go ye therefore, and teach all nations, baptizing them in the name of the Father, and of the Son, and of the Holy Ghost: Teaching them to observe all things whatsoever I have commanded you: and, lo, I am with you alway, even unto the end of the world. Amen.

Matthew 28:19

The final instructions of our Savior during His earthly ministry did not have to do with how to have church. He did not close this chapter of time with instructions on marriage or family planning. Some would have you believe that the most important thing Jesus ever discussed was money, but at His moment of departure, it was not finance on His mind. The truth of the matter is that the final instructions of Christ centered on the advancement of His Kingdom.

He lays out what Kingdom advancement looks like to Him, and when I see what it has become in the modern Church, particularly here in the West, I am grateful that He did not completely remove His Spirit from the Church. There is nothing in this passage about large buildings or great amounts of staff, nor do I find any admonishment in the text to produce high-traffic, low-impact conferences that preach only the message of Dr. Doolittle and Rev. I. Feelgoode. Instead, our Lord left us with instructions to teach.

So simple and pure is the heart of the Savior that up to His last earthly moments, His admonishment was to elevate the thoughts of people. The start His ministry is a message of repentance, which at the opening of this book we discovered it is really a message to elevate our minds and thinking. Christ seals His ministry with a call to us who have repented to take the message of the elevation of thought to others, and to show the world what has transformed our lives. The challenge to us today is to empower someone through the Word to activate metacognition in their own mind and spirit, which they too might think with the mind of Christ.

The promise He leaves with us is that in our process of pointing minds to the revolutionary power of the Gospel of Christ, He will be with us. His Spirit empowering us to walk in wisdom and giving us access to His riches in glory is enough to challenge us to find someone to share this message with today.

My prayer for you is that through the Word of God, you have been encouraged, empowered, enlightened, and equipped for the work of the ministry. I pray that the words on these pages have found a place in your cognitive thought and that transformation is germinating in the womb of your spirit. May the grace of our Lord Jesus Christ, and the sweet communion of His Holy Spirit, rest, rule, and abide in your heart both now and forever more. Amen.

[1]*The Holy Bible: King James Version.* 1995. Logos Research Systems, Inc.: Oak Harbor, WA
[2]Strong, J. 1996. *The exhaustive concordance of the Bible: Showing every word of the test of the common English version of the canonical books, and every occurrence of each word in regular order.* (electronic ed.) . Woodside Bible Fellowship.: Ontario
[3]Strong, J. 1996. *The exhaustive concordance of the Bible: Showing every word of the test of the common English version of the canonical books, and every occurrence of each word in regular order.* (electronic ed.) . Woodside Bible Fellowship.: Ontario
[4]Young, R. 1997. *Young's literal translation.* Logos Research Systems: Oak Harbor
[5]Strong, J. 1996. *The exhaustive concordance of the Bible: Showing every word of the test of the common English version of the canonical books, and every occurrence of each word in regular order.* (electronic ed.) . Woodside Bible Fellowship.: Ontario
[6]*The Holy Bible: King James Version.* 1995. Logos Research Systems, Inc.: Oak Harbor, WA
[7]Strong, J. 1996. *The exhaustive concordance of the Bible: Showing every word of the test of the common English version of the canonical books, and every occurrence of each word in regular order.* (electronic ed.) . Woodside Bible Fellowship.: Ontario
[8]Strong, J. 1996. *The exhaustive concordance of the Bible: Showing every word of the test of the common English version of the canonical books, and every occurrence of each word in regular order.* (electronic ed.) . Woodside Bible Fellowship.: Ontario
[9]Strong, J. 1996. *The exhaustive concordance of the Bible: Showing every word of the test of the common English version of the canonical books, and every occurrence of each word In regular order.* (electronic ed.) . Woodside Bible Fellowship.: Ontario
[10]*The Holy Bible: King James Version.* 1995. Logos Research Systems, Inc.: Oak Harbor, WA

[11]*The Holy Bible: King James Version.* 1995. Logos Research Systems, Inc.: Oak Harbor, WA
[12]Young, R. 1997. *Young's literal translation.* Logos Research Systems: Oak Harbor
[13]Young, R. 1997. *Young's literal translation.* Logos Research Systems: Oak Harbor
[14]Young, R. 1997. *Young's literal translation.* Logos Research Systems: Oak Harbor
[15]*The Holy Bible: King James Version.* 1995. Logos Research Systems, Inc.: Oak Harbor, WA
[16]Strong, J. 1996. *The exhaustive concordance of the Bible: Showing every word of the test of the common English version of the canonical books, and every occurrence of each word in regular order.* (electronic ed.) . Woodside Bible Fellowship.: Ontario
[17]Strong, J. 1996. *The exhaustive concordance of the Bible: Showing every word of the test of the common English version of the canonical books, and every occurrence of each word in regular order.* (electronic ed.) . Woodside Bible Fellowship.: Ontario
[18]Young, R. 1997. *Young's literal translation.* Logos Research Systems: Oak Harbor
[19]Young, R. 1997. *Young's literal translation.* Logos Research Systems: Oak Harbor
[20]Strong, J. 1996. *The exhaustive concordance of the Bible: Showing every word of the test of the common English version of the canonical books, and every occurrence of each word in regular order.* (electronic ed.) . Woodside Bible Fellowship.: Ontario
[21]Young, R. 1997. *Young's literal translation.* Logos Research Systems: Oak Harbor
[22]Merriam-Webster, I. 1996, c1993. *Merriam-Webster's collegiate dictionary.* Includes index. (10th ed.). Merriam-Webster: Springfield, Mass., U.S.A.
[23]Young, R. 1997. *Young's literal translation.* Logos Research Systems: Oak Harbor
[24]*The New King James Version.* 1996, c1982. Thomas Nelson: Nashville
[25]Young, R. 1997. *Young's literal translation.* Logos Research Systems: Oak Harbor

[26]Young, R. 1997. *Young's literal translation.* Logos Research Systems: Oak Harbor

[27]*The Holy Bible: King James Version.* 1995. Logos Research Systems, Inc.: Oak Harbor, WA

[28]Strong, J. 1996. *The exhaustive concordance of the Bible: Showing every word of the test of the common English version of the canonical books, and every occurrence of each word in regular order.* (electronic ed.) . Woodside Bible Fellowship.: Ontario

[29]Strong, J. 1996. *The exhaustive concordance of the Bible: Showing every word of the test of the common English version of the canonical books, and every occurrence of each word in regular order.* (electronic ed.) . Woodside Bible Fellowship.: Ontario

[30]Strong, J. 1996. *The exhaustive concordance of the Bible: Showing every word of the test of the common English version of the canonical books, and every occurrence of each word in regular order.* (electronic ed.) . Woodside Bible Fellowship.: Ontario

[31]Strong, J. 1996. *The exhaustive concordance of the Bible: Showing every word of the test of the common English version of the canonical books, and every occurrence of each word in regular order.* (electronic ed.) . Woodside Bible Fellowship.: Ontario

[32]*The New King James Version.* 1996, c1982. Thomas Nelson: Nashville

[33]*The Holy Bible: King James Version.* 1995. Logos Research Systems, Inc.: Oak Harbor, WA

[34]*The Holy Bible: King James Version.* 1995. Logos Research Systems, Inc.: Oak Harbor, WA

[35]Young, R. 1997. *Young's literal translation.* Logos Research Systems: Oak Harbor

[36]Strong, J. 1996. *The exhaustive concordance of the Bible: Showing every word of the test of the common English version of the canonical books, and every occurrence of each word in regular order.* (electronic ed.) . Woodside Bible Fellowship.: Ontario

[37]Strong, J. 1996. *The exhaustive concordance of the Bible: Showing every word of the test of the common English version of the canonical books, and every occurrence of each word in regular order.* (electronic ed.) . Woodside Bible Fellowship.: Ontario

[38]*The Holy Bible: King James Version.* 1995. Logos Research Systems, Inc.: Oak Harbor, WA
[39]Strong, J. 1996. *The exhaustive concordance of the Bible: Showing every word of the test of the common English version of the canonical books, and every occurrence of each word in regular order.* (electronic ed.) . Woodside Bible Fellowship.: Ontario
[40]Young, R. 1997. *Young's literal translation.* Logos Research Systems: Oak Harbor

Made in the USA
Monee, IL
08 November 2026

67384890R10046